DISCOVERING

TALLINN **2023**

"unveiling the Hidden Treasures, Rich History, and
Enchanting Charm of Estonia's Historic Capital"

SCOTT WEST

Tallinn Brief Facts

Location: Tallinn is the capital city of Estonia, located on the northern coast of the country along the Baltic Sea.

Currency: The currency used in Tallinn is the Euro (EUR).

Capital: Tallinn is the capital and largest city of Estonia.

Time zone: Tallinn follows Eastern European Time (EET), which is UTC+2 during Standard Time and UTC+3 during Daylight Saving Time.

Population: The population of Tallinn is approximately 450,000, making it the most populous city in Estonia.

Language: The official language of Tallinn is Estonian, but English is widely spoken, especially in tourist areas.

Climate: Tallinn experiences a humid continental climate with mild summers and cold winters, with average temperatures ranging from 20°C (68°F) in summer to -5°C (23°F) in winter.

Crime: Tallinn is generally considered safe for travelers, but it is always recommended to take normal precautions against petty theft and stay aware of your surroundings.

Current voltage: The electrical voltage in Tallinn is 230 volts, with a frequency of 50 Hz, and the standard plug type is the European CEE 7/5 (Schuko) plug.

The people: The people of Tallinn are known for their hospitality and friendliness, welcoming visitors from around the world with warmth and openness.

Food: Estonian cuisine in Tallinn offers a mix of traditional dishes like black bread, smoked fish, and sauerkraut, as well as international flavors and modern culinary innovations.

TABLE OF CONTENTS

FOREWORD
    OVERVIEW
    LOCATION AND GEOGRAPHICAL
    HISTORY AND CULTURAL SIGNIFICANCE
CHAPTER 1:
EXPLORING THE OLD TOWN
    Medieval Architecture and Landmarks
    Toompea Hill and Viewing Points
    Alexander Nevsky Cathedral
    Town Hall Square (Raekoja plats)
CHAPTER 2:
MUSEUMS AND CULTURAL EXPERIENCES
    Estonian History Museum
    Kumu Art Museum
    Seaplane Harbour Maritime Museum
    Kadriorg Palace and Park
CHAPTER 3:
TALLINN'S MODERN ATTRACTIONS
    Telliskivi Creative City
    Rotermann Quarter
    Tallinn TV Tower
    Estonian Open Air Museum
CHAPTER 4:
PARKS, GARDENS, AND NATURE
    Kadriorg Park
    Pirita Promenade and Beach

Lahemaa National Park

Botanic Garden of Tallinn

CHAPTER 5:

CUISINE AND DINING

Traditional Estonian Dishes

Local Markets and Food Halls

Top-Rated Restaurants and Cafes

Craft Beer and Distilleries

CHAPTER 6:

LANGUAGE GUIDE

Basic Estonian Phrases and Expressions

Pronunciation Guide

Useful Vocabulary for Travelers

Language Tips and Etiquette

CHAPTER 7:

DAY TRIPS AND NEARBY ATTRACTIONS

Helsinki, Finland

Lahemaa National Park

Saaremaa Island

Paldiski and Pakri Peninsula

CHAPTER 8:

PRACTICAL INFORMATION FOR VISITORS

Getting to Tallinn

Transportation within the City

Accommodation Options

Travel Tips and Essential Information

Currency, Language, and Safety

Local Customs and Etiquette

Emergency Contacts

Additional Resources

CHAPTER 9:

SHOPPING AND SOUVENIRS

    Old Town Souvenir Shops

    Viru Keskus Shopping Center

    Estonian Design and Handicrafts

CHAPTER 10:

FAMILY-FRIENDLY ACTIVITIES

    Tallinn Zoo

    Lennusadam Kids' Area

    Nõmme Adventure Park

CHAPTER 11:

SPORTS AND RECREATION

    Water Activities and Beaches

    Skiing and Winter Sports

    Golf Courses and Sports Facilities

CHAPTER 12:

TALLINN'S NIGHTLIFE

    Bars and Pubs

    Live Music Venues

    Nightclubs and Dancing

CHAPTER 13:

SUSTAINABLE TOURISM IN TALLINN

    Eco-Friendly Practices and Initiatives

    Parks and Green Spaces

    Responsible Travel Tips

CHAPTER 14:

CALENDAR OF EVENTS (for the year 2023)

    Major Festivals and Celebrations

    Cultural and Art Events

    Sports Events and Competitions

    CONCLUSION AND FINAL THOUGHT

FOREWORD

Tallinn, Estonia's charming capital city, is a destination for visitors who are fascinated by its fascinating history, beautiful historical town, and lively atmosphere. As someone who has experienced the wonders of Tallinn firsthand, I can attest to its unique allure and the warm hospitality of its people.

It's like entering a fairy tale when you step into Tallinn. A UNESCO World Heritage site, Old Town transports you back in time with its cobblestone streets, medieval architecture, and preserved city walls. You'll find a rich tapestry of colorful buildings, quaint shops, and trendy cafes as you make your way down the short alleyways. The atmosphere is lively, but there's a sense of tranquility that flows in the air.

Every stone and corner is filled with Tallinn's history. The city's architectural gems are displayed proudly, from the magnificent Alexander Nevsky Cathedral with its onion dome to the grandness of Town Hall Square. Toompea Hill, with its stunning scenic views, offers a glance into Tallinn's past as a medieval stronghold.

Beyond its historical charm, Tallinn embraces the present with open arms. In a city where innovation and creativity flourish, it has taken on the role of a leading technology hub. Modern neighborhoods like Telliskivi Creative City and Rotermann Quarter blend contemporary design with industrial heritage, housing trendy boutiques, hip cafes, and art galleries.

Tallinn is also Estonia's cultural capital, where some numerous museums and galleries display the country's rich heritage and art. A view of the past and current state of Estonia can be found at both Estonian History Museum and Kumu Art Museum. At Seaplane Harbour, a museum devoted to maritime history in this part of the Region is set up and Kadriorg Palace and Park offers a peaceful retreat decorated by beautiful gardens and impressive paintings.

When it comes to culinary delights, Tallinn does not disappoint. The city boasts a vibrant food scene that celebrates both traditional Estonian cuisine and international flavors. You can indulge in hearty dishes like black bread, marinated herring, and elk stew, or savor gourmet meals at Michelin-starred restaurants that fuse local ingredients with contemporary techniques. Don't miss the chance to visit local markets, such as the Balti Jaama Turg, to discover fresh produce, artisanal products, and traditional treats.

For nature lovers, Tallinn offers a refreshing escape. Parks and green spaces, like Kadriorg Park and Pirita Promenade, provide peaceful retreats for leisure and outdoor activities. If you're up for an adventure, the nearby Lahemaa National Park beckons with its pristine forests, picturesque coastal areas, and historic manor houses.

Tallinn's charm extends beyond its borders, as day trips to Helsinki, Finland, or exploring the breathtaking beauty of the nearby Saaremaa Island and Paldiski Peninsula are within easy reach. The city's accessibility and efficient transportation system make it convenient to explore both Tallinn and its surroundings.

Whether you're walking through the medieval streets of the Old Town, immersing yourself in cultural experiences, indulging in culinary delights, or discovering the natural wonders surrounding the city, Tallinn leaves an indelible mark on every visitor. Its seamless blend of history and modernity, coupled with the warmth and welcoming nature of its people, make it a truly unforgettable destination. So, come and discover the magic of Tallinn for yourself, and allow this city to weave its spell around you.

OVERVIEW

Tallinn, the capital city of Estonia, is a charming and lively destination that offers an exciting mix of history, culture as well as modern trends. Tallinn, situated on Estonia's north coast, is a reminder of the country's strong heritage and its embrace of progress. Tallinn has a wealth of things for all visitors to see and enjoy, thanks to its richly preserved

Middle Ages Old Town, lively contemporary villages as well as delightful countryside.

The city exudes a unique atmosphere that seamlessly merges its historical roots with contemporary life. Tallinn's Old Town, a UNESCO World Heritage site, is a labyrinth of narrow cobblestone streets, medieval buildings, and Gothic spires. This well-preserved medieval city center invites exploration and transports visitors back in time, offering a glimpse into Tallinn's past as a trading hub of the Hanseatic League. The city's rich history and architectural beauty have earned it the nickname "The Medieval Pearl."

Beyond the Old Town, Tallinn has embraced modernity with open arms. The city is renowned for its thriving tech and startup scene, earning it the moniker "Estonian Silicon Valley." Tallinn boasts a progressive and innovative spirit, with modern neighborhoods like Telliskivi Creative City and Rotermann Quarter serving as creative hubs that blend art, design, and technology. These areas are teeming with trendy shops, galleries, and cafes, providing a vibrant and contemporary contrast to the historical charm of the Old Town.

LOCATION AND GEOGRAPHICAL

Tallinn is situated on the southern Gulf of Finland's coast, which faces Helsinki's capital city in the Baltic Sea. This is located in the northern part of Estonia and it serves as a strategically important hub for connections both at local and global levels. Historically, the town's favorable location has contributed to its growth as an important trading hub and a melting pot of cultures.

Surrounded by natural beauty, Tallinn benefits from its proximity to lush forests, scenic coastline, and picturesque landscapes.

The city enjoys a maritime climate, with mild summers and relatively cold winters. The changing seasons bring a unique charm to Tallinn, with each offering distinct experiences for visitors.

HISTORY AND CULTURAL SIGNIFICANCE

Tallinn's history spans over eight centuries, and its cultural heritage reflects the influences of various civilizations. Originally settled by the Estonians, Tallinn later saw the arrival of German, Danish, Swedish, and

Russian rulers, each leaving their mark on the city's architecture, traditions, and cultural identity.

During the medieval period, Tallinn flourished as a bustling Hanseatic trading city, known for its prosperity and commercial connections throughout Europe. The city's well-preserved medieval structures, such as the fortified city walls, towers, and merchant houses, bear witness to this prosperous era.

Tallinn's history took a turn with the Soviet occupation during the 20th century.

However, since Estonia regained its independence in 1991, Tallinn has undergone a remarkable transformation, revitalizing its cultural heritage and embracing its role as a dynamic European capital.

Tallinn's ability to seamlessly merge its past with its current identity is now an important feature of the city's culture. Estonia's cultural achievements are celebrated and its contemporary creativity is made visible in the lively arts scene of this city, a large collection of museums as well as annual festivals. Estonia's cultural institutions, such as the Estonian History Museum and Kumu Art Gallery, give us an insight into this country's past and present, making Tallinn a major center of culture and national pride.

With its captivating history, diverse cultural heritage, and thriving arts scene, Tallinn is a destination that captivates and enlightens visitors, offering a glimpse into Estonia's past and its vibrant present.

CHAPTER 1:

EXPLORING THE OLD TOWN

There is a treasure chest of medieval architecture, historic treasures, and charming cobblestone streets in Tallinn's Old Town. It is a step back in time for you to explore this UNESCO World Heritage site and take an interest in the rich history and charming atmosphere of the town.

Medieval Architecture and Landmarks

The Old Town of Tallinn boasts an impressive collection of medieval architecture that has been exceptionally well-preserved over the centuries. As you wander through the narrow streets, you'll encounter a variety of architectural styles, including Gothic, Romanesque, and Baroque influences.

One of the most iconic landmarks is the Tallinn City Wall, which surrounds the Old Town and stretches for approximately 2 kilometers. This fortified wall, complete with towers and gates, is a testament to Tallinn's medieval past and provides a glimpse into the city's defensive history.

The Tallinn Town Hall, located in the heart of the Old Town's Town Hall Square (Raekoja plats), is another remarkable architectural gem. This Gothic-style building dates back to the 13th century and has served as a symbol of Tallinn's self-governance throughout the centuries. The Town Hall houses a museum where you can learn more about the city's history and admire its grand halls and historic artifacts.

Other notable landmarks in the Old Town include St. Olaf's Church, a towering structure that was once one of the tallest buildings in the world, and the Great Guild Hall, an imposing Gothic-style building that now serves as a venue for concerts and events. The Dominican Monastery, with its beautiful cloister, and the St. Catherine's Passage, a charming alley lined with artisan workshops, are also worth exploring.

Toompea Hill and Viewing Points

Rising above the Old Town, Toompea Hill offers breathtaking panoramic views of Tallinn and the surrounding areas. This historic hill is home to several important landmarks, including the Estonian Parliament (Riigikogu) and the Toompea Castle.

Toompea Castle, dating back to the 13th century, houses the offices of the Estonian Parliament and the Prime Minister. Its distinctive pink facade and tall towers make it a prominent landmark visible from various parts of the city. Visitors can explore the castle grounds and enjoy the picturesque views from the viewing platforms.

Another popular viewpoint on Toompea Hill is the Kohtuotsa Viewing Platform. From here, you can admire the panoramic vistas of the Old Town, the Baltic Sea, and the modern skyline of Tallinn. The viewing platform provides a perfect spot for capturing memorable photos and appreciating the city's beauty from above.

Alexander Nevsky Cathedral

The Alexander Nevsky Cathedral is an iconic symbol of Tallinn and a testament to the city's diverse history. This Russian Orthodox cathedral, built in the late 19th century, showcases an impressive combination of Russian architectural elements, including its distinctive onion domes and ornate facade.

Step inside the cathedral to admire the beautiful iconostasis, intricate mosaics, and stunning interior decorations. The cathedral holds religious services and offers visitors a chance to learn about the Orthodox faith and its significance to the local Russian community.

Town Hall Square (Raekoja plats)

Town Hall Square, or Raekoja Plats, is the bustling heart of the Old Town and a gathering place for locals and visitors alike. This lively square is surrounded by colorful merchant houses, outdoor cafes, and historic landmarks, creating a vibrant and captivating atmosphere.

The centerpiece of the square is the Tallinn Town Hall, a magnificent Gothic building that dates back to the 15th century. Its iconic spire, adorned with a weather vane known as "Old Thomas," has become a symbol of Tallinn. The square is a hub of activity, hosting various events throughout the year, including the popular Christmas Market.

While at Town Hall Square, take a moment to soak in the ambiance, enjoy a cup of coffee at one of the charming cafes, and admire the architecture that surrounds you. The square serves as a starting point for exploring the Old Town, with its narrow streets leading to hidden corners and delightful discoveries.

Exploring the Old Town of Tallinn is like stepping into a living history book. From its medieval architecture and landmarks to the stunning views from Toompea Hill and the grandeur of the Alexander Nevsky Cathedral, every corner of this enchanting district tells a story of the city's past and offers a memorable experience for all who visit.

CHAPTER 2:

MUSEUMS AND CULTURAL EXPERIENCES

Tallinn's a city that upholds its cultural heritage and offers an extensive collection of museums as well as historical experiences for tourists. These cultural institutions offer fascinating glimpses into the past and present of Estonia, from studying Estonian history to immersing oneself in contemporary art.

Estonian History Museum

The Estonian History Museum, located within the Great Guild Hall in Tallinn's Old Town, is a must-visit for history enthusiasts. The museum offers a comprehensive overview of Estonia's past, spanning from ancient times to the present day. Through engaging exhibitions and interactive displays, visitors can gain a deeper understanding of the country's historical events, cultural development, and national identity.

Explore the diverse galleries that showcase artifacts, photographs, and multimedia presentations, offering a captivating journey through time. Learn about Estonia's struggle for independence, its Soviet era, and its remarkable transformation into a modern European nation. The Estonian History Museum provides an educational and thought-provoking experience that helps to contextualize the rich heritage of Tallinn and Estonia as a whole.

Kumu Art Museum

The Kumu Art Museum, situated in the beautiful Kadriorg Park, is the largest and most prestigious art museum in Estonia. It houses a remarkable collection of Estonian art from the 18th century to the present day, showcasing a wide range of styles and artistic expressions.

The museum's permanent collection features works by renowned Estonian artists, offering a glimpse into the nation's artistic evolution over the centuries. From classic landscapes and portraits to contemporary installations and multimedia art, the exhibits at Kumu provide a comprehensive overview of Estonian art history.

In addition to the permanent collection, Kumu hosts temporary exhibitions that showcase international contemporary art and provide a platform for dialogue and artistic exchange. The museum's architecture itself is a work of art, blending modern design with the historic surroundings of Kadriorg Park.

Seaplane Harbour Maritime Museum

For those interested in maritime history, the Seaplane Harbour Maritime Museum is a fascinating destination. Housed in a historic seaplane hangar near Tallinn Bay, the museum offers a captivating journey through Estonia's maritime heritage.

Explore the extensive collection of ships, submarines, and seaplanes that played significant roles in Estonia's maritime past. Step aboard a full-scale replica of a historic submarine or walk the decks of a century-old steam-powered icebreaker. The museum's interactive exhibits bring maritime history to life, allowing visitors to experience the challenges faced by sailors and explorers of the past.

The Seaplane Harbour Maritime Museum also delves into the technological advancements that have shaped Estonia's maritime industry. From navigational instruments to shipbuilding innovations, the museum showcases the country's contributions to maritime technology.

Kadriorg Palace and Park

Kadriorg Palace, located in the picturesque Kadriorg Park, is a testament to the grandeur of Estonian architecture and art. Built-in the 18th century by Peter the Great of Russia, the palace is a stunning example of Baroque architecture and serves as a cultural landmark.

Step inside the palace to admire its beautifully decorated rooms, which house the collections of the Art Museum of Estonia. The palace features a diverse range of art, including European paintings, sculptures, and decorative arts from the 16th to the 20th century. Explore the exhibitions that showcase both international masterpieces and Estonian artists, providing a glimpse into the artistic influences that have shaped the nation's cultural identity.

Surrounding the palace, Kadriorg Park offers a peaceful retreat from the bustling city. Stroll through the manicured gardens, enjoy the serene water features, and discover hidden pathways that lead to charming corners of tranquility. The park is also home to the Kumu Art Museum, providing visitors with the opportunity to combine cultural experiences in one scenic location.

Tallinn's museums and cultural experiences offer a fascinating glimpse into the country's history, art, and maritime heritage. Whether you're interested in delving into Estonia's past at the Estonian History Museum, exploring the vibrant contemporary art scene at Kumu, immersing yourself in maritime history at the Seaplane Harbour Maritime Museum, or admiring the grandeur of Kadriorg Palace and Park, Tallinn provides a rich cultural tapestry for visitors to discover and enjoy.

CHAPTER 3:

TALLINN'S MODERN ATTRACTIONS

Even though the city of Tallinn is well known for its historical and medieval charm, it also has a lively and contemporary feel to it. These contemporary sights reveal Tallinn's dynamic spirit, and its embrace of the present, from creative centers to architectural marvels.

Telliskivi Creative City

Telliskivi Creative City is a thriving cultural and creative hub located just outside the Old Town of Tallinn. This former industrial complex has been transformed into a lively neighborhood filled with art studios, galleries, boutiques, restaurants, and event spaces.

The area pulsates with creativity, providing a platform for local artists, designers, and entrepreneurs to showcase their talents. Wander through the graffiti-adorned streets, explore the unique shops and galleries, and indulge in a diverse range of cuisine offered by the numerous cafes and restaurants.

Telliskivi Creative City is not just a place to shop and dine; it also hosts regular cultural events, live music performances, art exhibitions, and festivals. It's a dynamic and ever-changing space that captures the contemporary essence of Tallinn's creative scene.

Rotermann Quarter

The Rotermann Quarter is a fascinating blend of history and modernity, seamlessly combining old industrial buildings with contemporary architecture. Located between the Old Town and the city center, this revitalized neighborhood is a testament to Tallinn's urban regeneration efforts.

The quarter is characterized by its striking mix of restored factory buildings and modern glass-and-steel structures. It houses trendy boutiques, design studios, cafes, restaurants, and office spaces, creating a vibrant atmosphere for both locals and visitors.

Explore the narrow streets and courtyards of the Rotermann Quarter, where you'll find a fusion of architectural styles and a variety of shops and eateries. From fashion boutiques and design stores to gourmet food markets and cozy cafes, the quarter offers a modern and stylish experience.

Tallinn TV Tower

For breathtaking views and a thrilling experience, a visit to the Tallinn TV Tower is a must. Standing tall at 314 meters, it is the tallest structure in Estonia and offers panoramic vistas of the city and its surroundings.

Take an elevator to the observation deck, located at a height of 170 meters, and marvel at the stunning views of Tallinn's skyline, the Baltic Sea, and the picturesque landscapes beyond. On a clear day, you can even see the Gulf of Finland and Helsinki.

The Tallinn TV Tower also offers a range of interactive exhibits and displays, allowing visitors to learn about the tower's construction, the history of television broadcasting, and the significant events that have taken place in the tower's observation deck.

Estonian Open Air Museum

Located on the outskirts of Tallinn, the Estonian Open Air Museum provides a glimpse into the rural life and cultural heritage of Estonia. Set in a sprawling outdoor area, the museum showcases traditional farmsteads, wooden windmills, village churches, and other historical buildings that have been preserved and relocated from various parts of the country.

Stroll through the museum's picturesque landscapes and explore the different regions of Estonia represented in the exhibits. Engage with costumed guides who demonstrate traditional crafts and activities, providing insights into the daily lives of Estonian peasants throughout history.

The museum also hosts events and festivals that celebrate Estonian traditions, such as Midsummer's Day and Christmas festivities, offering visitors a chance to experience the country's cultural heritage in an immersive and interactive way.

Tallinn's modern attractions provide a contrast to the city's historic charm, offering visitors a chance to explore the contemporary side of Estonia's capital. Whether you're discovering the creative energy of Telliskivi Creative City, admiring the architectural fusion of Rotermann Quarter, enjoying panoramic views from the

Tallinn TV Tower, or immersing yourself in the rural traditions at the Estonian Open Air Museum, these modern attractions contribute to the diverse and dynamic tapestry of Tallinn's cultural landscape.

CHAPTER 4:

PARKS, GARDENS, AND NATURE

Tallinn's not only a city of history and culture but also a town that shares nature's beauty. There are plenty of opportunities to connect with nature and enjoy the outdoors in and around Tallinn, from beautiful parks and gardens to serene coastal areas and extensive national parks.

Kadriorg Park

Kadriorg Park is a verdant oasis located just a short distance from Tallinn's city center. This picturesque park is known for its well-manicured lawns, beautiful flower beds, and tranquil atmosphere. It was established in the 18th century by Peter the Great of Russia as a summer residence for his wife, Catherine I.

Take a stroll along the park's winding paths, enjoy a picnic on the grassy meadows, or simply relax in the shade of the tall trees. The park is home to several notable attractions, including the stunning Kadriorg Palace and the Kumu Art Museum. It also features ponds, fountains, and sculptures that add to its charm.

Pirita Promenade and Beach

For those seeking a coastal retreat, Pirita Promenade and Beach offer a refreshing escape from the urban bustle of Tallinn. Stretching along the Pirita River and the Gulf of Finland, this scenic promenade is a popular spot for leisurely walks, jogging, and cycling.

The promenade offers breathtaking views of the sea, with sailboats dotting the horizon. You can also enjoy a relaxing day at Pirita Beach, which features sandy shores and designated swimming areas during the summer months. The beach is perfect for sunbathing, building sandcastles, or taking a refreshing dip in the Baltic Sea.

Lahemaa National Park

For nature enthusiasts and adventure seekers, a visit to Lahemaa National Park is highly recommended. Located just a short drive from Tallinn, this expansive national park is a haven of natural beauty, diverse landscapes, and rich biodiversity.

Explore the park's pristine forests, picturesque coastal cliffs, and serene lakes. Discover the charm of traditional Estonian fishing villages nestled along the coast. Hike along nature trails that lead you through dense forests, past waterfalls, and scenic viewpoints.

Lahemaa National Park is also home to historical manor houses, such as Palmse

Manor and Sagadi Manor, which provide a glimpse into Estonia's noble past. The park offers a range of outdoor activities, including hiking, birdwatching, and canoeing, allowing visitors to immerse themselves in the natural wonders of Estonia.

Botanic Garden of Tallinn

Located in the Kloostrimetsa neighborhood, the Botanic Garden of Tallinn is a paradise for plant lovers. This green oasis spans over 123 hectares and features an impressive collection of plants from Estonia and around the world.

Wander through the garden's various sections, including the alpine garden, rose garden, arboretum, and rock garden. Admire the vibrant colors and fragrant aromas of flowers in bloom, and learn about the diverse plant species that thrive in different ecosystems.

The Botanic Garden of Tallinn is not only a place of natural beauty but also an educational institution that conducts research, conservation efforts, and educational programs. It serves as a peaceful retreat where visitors can reconnect with nature and gain a deeper appreciation for the botanical wonders of the world.

Tallinn's parks, gardens, and natural attractions offer a refreshing escape and a chance to appreciate the beauty of the outdoors. Whether you're exploring the serene Kadriorg Park, enjoying the coastal views at Pirita Promenade and Beach, immersing yourself in the wilderness of Lahemaa National Park, or discovering the botanical treasures at the Botanic Garden of Tallinn, nature lovers will find a wealth of experiences to enjoy in and around the city.

CHAPTER 5:

CUISINE AND DINING

The culinary scene in Tallinn is a fine mix of traditional Estonian flavors, international influences, and the growing culture of craft beers and distilleries. There is something to satisfy all tastes, whether it's fine Estonian cuisine or exploring local markets and enjoying the finest restaurants and cafés.

Traditional Estonian Dishes

Immerse yourself in the flavors of Estonia by sampling traditional dishes that have been passed down through generations. Some must-try Estonian specialties include:

a) **Sült (Jellied Meat):** A dish made from boiled and seasoned meat, typically pork, set in a gelatinous broth. It is often served cold as an appetizer.

b) **Verivorst (Blood Sausage):** A sausage made from pork blood, barley, and various spices. It is typically enjoyed during the Christmas season.

c) **Mulgikapsad (Mulgian Cabbage):** A hearty dish made from sauerkraut, pork, and potatoes, often flavored with caraway seeds.

d) **Kama:** A traditional Estonian dessert made from roasted and milled grains, usually served with yogurt or buttermilk.

e) **Smoked Fish:** Estonia's location on the Baltic Sea means there is an abundance of smoked fish available, including salmon, herring, and eel. Enjoy it on rye bread with traditional toppings like red onion and sour cream.

Local Markets and Food Halls

To experience the vibrant food culture of Tallinn, head to the local markets and food halls where you can find fresh produce, regional delicacies, and artisanal products. Some popular options include:

a) **Balti Jaama Turg (Baltic Station Market):** Located near the train station, this market offers a wide range of local produce, meat, fish, dairy products, and handicrafts. Explore the stalls and enjoy a variety of street food options.

b) **Kalamaja Food Market:** Situated in the trendy Kalamaja district, this market showcases local vendors selling organic produce, homemade bread, cheeses, and other delectable treats.

c) **Telliskivi Flea Market:** While primarily a flea market, it also features food stalls where you can taste local snacks and street food favorites.

d) **Rahva Toit Food Hall:** This modern food hall in the heart of Tallinn offers a variety of cuisines, including Estonian, Asian, and Mediterranean. Indulge in diverse flavors and culinary delights from different cultures.

Top-Rated Restaurants and Cafes

Tallinn boasts a vibrant dining scene with numerous top-rated restaurants and cozy cafes. Here are a few recommendations:

a) **Rataskaevu 16:** Located in the heart of the Old Town, this restaurant is renowned for its classic Estonian dishes, warm atmosphere, and excellent service. Try their famous elk soup or traditional sauerkraut with pork.

b) **NOA Restoran:** Situated by the sea in Pirita, NOA Restoran offers a fine dining experience with panoramic views. Their menu showcases innovative Estonian cuisine, focusing on local and seasonal ingredients.

c) **F-hoone:** Housed in a former industrial building in Kalamaja, F-hoone combines a laid-back atmosphere with delicious food. Enjoy their selection of burgers, salads, and Estonian comfort food.

d) **Kohvik Must Puudel:** This charming café in the Old Town serves up delicious breakfast options, freshly baked pastries, and a cozy atmosphere. It's an ideal spot to start your day with a cup of coffee and a hearty meal.

Craft Beer and Distilleries

Tallinn has a burgeoning craft beer and distillery scene, with establishments that offer unique flavors and local brews. Some notable places to explore include:

a) **Põhjala Brewery:** Located in the Bohemian Kalamaja district, Põhjala Brewery is known for its innovative craft beers. Visit their taproom to sample a variety of brews and learn about the brewing process.

b) **Koch Distillery:** Situated in the heart of Tallinn, Koch Distillery produces a range of high-quality spirits, including gin and vodka. Take a guided tour to discover their distillation methods and enjoy tastings of their handcrafted products.

As you explore Tallinn's culinary offerings, don't miss the opportunity to indulge in traditional Estonian dishes, explore the local markets, dine at top-rated restaurants, and savor the unique flavors of craft beer and spirits. Each culinary experience offers a delightful glimpse into the rich gastronomic heritage of Estonia.

CHAPTER 6:

LANGUAGE GUIDE

You can familiarize yourself with some of Estonia's common phrases and expressions, comprehend the pronunciation, acquire a good vocabulary during your visit to Tallinn, as well as be aware of language guidelines and etiquette. In addition, we have prepared a language guide for you to use during your travels:

Basic Estonian Phrases and Expressions

Learning a few key phrases in Estonian can go a long way in enhancing your travel experience and interacting with the locals. Here are some essential phrases to get you started:

- Tere! (Hello!)
- Palun (Please)
- Aitäh (Thank you)
- Vabandage (Excuse me)
- Kuidas läheb? (How are you?)

- Kas sa räägid inglise keelt? (Do you speak English?)

- Kui palju see maksab? (How much does it cost?)

- Kas saaksite mind aidata? (Could you help me?)

- Nägemist! (Goodbye!)

Pronunciation Guide

Estonian pronunciation may be a bit challenging for non-native speakers. Here are a few guidelines to help you with the pronunciation:

a) The letters "ä," "ö," and "ü" have unique sounds. "Ä" is pronounced like the "a" in "cat," "ö" is similar to the "u" in "burn," and "ü" is similar to the French "u" or the German "ü."

b) Pay attention to stress. Estonian words are typically stressed on the first syllable. Practice the rolled "r" sound, as it is common in Estonian pronunciation.

Useful Vocabulary for Travelers

Having some basic vocabulary at your disposal can be beneficial while exploring Tallinn. Here are a few words and phrases that might come in handy:

- Hotell (Hotel)
- Restoran (Restaurant)
- Apteek (Pharmacy)
- Bussipeatus (Bus stop)
- Raha (Money)
- Rongijaam (Train station)
- Mida soovitate? (What do you recommend?)

- Tualett (Toilet)

- Pilet (Ticket)

Language Tips and Etiquette

Estonians appreciate when visitors make an effort to learn their language, even if only a few basic phrases. Here are some language tips and etiquette to keep in mind:

English is widely spoken in Tallinn, especially in tourist areas. However, learning a few Estonian phrases shows respect and can help you connect with the locals.

a) When addressing someone, use formal language unless you are in a casual setting or have been given permission to use informal language.

b) It's customary to greet people with a firm handshake while maintaining eye contact.

c) It's polite to say "Palun" (please) when making a request or ordering in a restaurant.

d) When entering a shop or a restaurant, it's customary to greet the staff with a friendly "Tere!" (Hello!).

e) Remember to thank people by saying "Aitäh" (Thank you) for their assistance or service.

By making an effort to learn a few basic Estonian phrases, understanding pronunciation, and following the local language tips and etiquette, you'll be able to navigate Tallinn with ease and show respect to the Estonian culture and people you encounter during your travels.

CHAPTER 7:

DAY TRIPS AND NEARBY ATTRACTIONS

While Tallinn is famous for its many wonders, there are several fascinating destinations close to the city that you should look into. Experience the beauty of Helsinki, the natural wonders of Lahemaa National Park, the peaceful Saaremaa Island, and the intriguing Paldiski and Pakri Peninsula on exciting day trips.

Helsinki, Finland

Just a short ferry ride away from Tallinn lies Helsinki, the capital of Finland. This vibrant city seamlessly blends modernity with a rich cultural heritage. Explore its architectural marvels, such as the iconic Helsinki Cathedral and the unique Rock Church (Temppeliaukio Church). Immerse yourself in Finnish design at the Design District and visit fascinating museums like the Ateneum and the Museum of Contemporary Art Kiasma. Don't miss the opportunity to indulge in Finnish cuisine and experience the sauna culture that Finland is renowned for.

Lahemaa National Park

For nature enthusiasts, a visit to Lahemaa National Park is a must. Located just east of Tallinn, this national park is a treasure trove of natural beauty. Explore its diverse landscapes, including pristine forests, picturesque coastal areas, and peaceful lakes. Discover charming manor houses, such as Palmse and Sagadi, which offer insights into Estonia's aristocratic past. Take a hike along the well-marked trails, go birdwatching, or simply relax in the tranquility of nature.

Saaremaa Island

Escape the hustle and bustle of the city and venture to Saaremaa Island, the largest island in Estonia. Known for its unspoiled natural beauty, Saaremaa offers a peaceful retreat with its idyllic countryside, sandy beaches, and charming villages. Visit the impressive Kuressaare Castle, explore the unique Kaali Meteorite Crater Field, and indulge in local delicacies, such as the renowned Saaremaa black bread and local honey. Saaremaa is also famous for its traditional windmills, which add to the island's enchanting atmosphere.

Paldiski and Pakri Peninsula

For a unique and historical day trip, consider visiting Paldiski and the Pakri Peninsula. Once a Soviet naval base, Paldiski bears witness to Estonia's complex past. Explore the remnants of the Soviet era, including the abandoned nuclear submarine training center. The nearby Pakri Peninsula offers stunning coastal cliffs, picturesque lighthouses, and hiking trails that showcase the region's natural beauty. It's an excellent destination for nature lovers and history enthusiasts alike.

These day trips and nearby attractions provide a wonderful opportunity to explore the diverse landscapes, cultural heritage, and neighboring countries around Tallinn. Whether you choose to immerse yourself in the cosmopolitan atmosphere of Helsinki, delve into the natural wonders of Lahemaa National Park, discover the tranquility of

Saaremaa Island, or unravel the historical remnants of Paldiski and the Pakri Peninsula, each destination promises a unique and unforgettable experience.

CHAPTER 8:

PRACTICAL INFORMATION FOR VISITORS

When planning a trip to Tallinn, it's essential to have practical information at your fingertips. Here is a guide to help you with getting to Tallinn, transportation within the city, accommodation options, travel tips, currency and language information, local customs, emergency contacts, and additional resources:

Getting to Tallinn

a) **By Air:** Tallinn is served by Lennart Meri Tallinn Airport (TLL), located just 4 kilometers from the city center. The airport offers connections to various European cities and beyond.

b) **By Ferry:** Tallinn has excellent ferry connections with neighboring countries, including Helsinki (Finland), Stockholm (Sweden), and St. Petersburg (Russia). The Tallinn Passenger Port is conveniently located near the city center.

Transportation within the City

a) **Public Transport:** Tallinn has an efficient public transportation system comprising buses, trams, and trolleys. Tickets can be purchased from the driver or through the mobile app. The Tallinn Card provides unlimited use of public transport.

b) **Taxis:** Taxis are widely available in Tallinn, and it's recommended to use licensed taxi services. Uber and Bolt are popular ride-hailing apps in the city.

Accommodation Options

Tallinn offers a range of accommodation options to suit different budgets and preferences. The city has a variety of hotels, guesthouses, hostels, and apartment rentals. The Old Town and city center are popular areas to stay in due to their proximity to major attractions.

Travel Tips and Essential Information

a) **Climate:** Tallinn has a temperate climate, with mild summers and cold winters. It's advisable to pack accordingly based on the season of your visit.

b) **Electricity:** The standard voltage is 230V, and the outlets accept Type F plugs.

c) **Safety:** Tallinn is generally a safe city, but it's always wise to take standard safety precautions, such as keeping an eye on your belongings and avoiding poorly lit or isolated areas at night.

d) **Tipping:** Tipping in Tallinn is appreciated but not mandatory. It's common to round up the bill or leave a small tip if you received good service.

Currency, Language, and Safety

a) **Currency:** The official currency in Estonia is the Euro (EUR). ATMs are widely available throughout the city, and credit cards are widely accepted.

b) **Language:** The official language of Estonia is Estonian. English is spoken by many locals, especially in tourist areas.

c) **Safety:** Tallinn is generally a safe city for travelers. However, it's always advisable to stay vigilant, keep an eye on your belongings, and be aware of your surroundings.

Local Customs and Etiquette

a) **Greeting:** When meeting someone, a handshake is a common form of greeting. Maintain eye contact and address people using their surnames unless invited to use their first name.

b) **Punctuality:** Estonians value punctuality, so it's polite to arrive on time for appointments and meetings.

c) **Table Manners:** When dining, it's customary to wait for the host to say "Tere tulemast!" (Welcome!) before starting the meal. It's also polite to finish everything on your plate.

Emergency Contacts

Emergency Services: In case of emergencies, dial 112. This number can be used for police, ambulance, or fire services.

Additional Resources

Visit Tallinn's official website: (www.visittallinn.ee)

Estonian Tourist Board:

(www.visitestonia.com)

These practical tips and essential information will help you navigate Tallinn with ease, ensuring a smooth and enjoyable travel experience. Remember to check official websites and local resources for the most up-to-date information before your trip.

CHAPTER 9:

SHOPPING AND SOUVENIRS

Tallinn offers a variety of shopping experiences, from charming souvenir shops in the Old Town to modern shopping centers and boutiques. Whether you're looking for traditional Estonian souvenirs, fashion, or unique handicrafts, here are some shopping destinations to explore:

Old Town Souvenir Shops

Exploring the narrow cobblestone streets of Tallinn's Old Town is an excellent opportunity to find unique souvenirs and gifts. The area is dotted with numerous shops offering traditional Estonian items, such as woolen clothing, handicrafts, ceramics, and amber jewelry. You'll also find plenty of marzipan shops, where you can purchase delicious marzipan treats shaped like fruits, animals, and landmarks.

Viru Keskus Shopping Center

For a modern shopping experience, head to Viru Keskus. Located in the heart of Tallinn, near the Old Town, this shopping center offers a wide range of international brands, designer boutiques, and department stores. You can browse through fashion, accessories, cosmetics, electronics, and more. Viru Keskus also houses various cafes and restaurants, providing a convenient spot to take a break and enjoy a meal.

Estonian Design and Handicrafts

If you're interested in Estonian design and handicrafts, there are several boutiques and galleries worth visiting. The Telliskivi Creative City, located just outside the Old Town, is a hub for creativity and innovation. It is home to numerous design shops and studios where you can find unique clothing, jewelry, home decor, and other artistic creations.

Additionally, the Estonian Design House, situated in the Rotermann Quarter, showcases a curated selection of locally designed products. Here, you can discover contemporary fashion, accessories, ceramics, furniture, and more, all created by talented Estonian designers.

For those seeking traditional handicrafts, the Masters' Courtyard (Meistrite Hoov) in the Old Town is a must-visit. This charming courtyard is home to several artisans who specialize in traditional Estonian crafts, such as ceramics, glassware, leatherwork, and textiles. You can watch the artisans at work and purchase unique handmade items directly from them.

When shopping for souvenirs or Estonian design products, keep an eye out for the "Estonian Design" or "Made in Estonia" labels, which indicate locally produced goods and support local artisans.

Tallinn's shopping scene offers a delightful mix of traditional and modern options, allowing you to find the perfect souvenirs, fashionable items, and unique Estonian designs. Whether you explore the souvenir shops in the Old Town, visit the Viru Keskus Shopping Center for international brands, or dive into the world of Estonian design and handicrafts, you're sure to find something special to take home.

CHAPTER 10:

FAMILY-FRIENDLY ACTIVITIES

Tallinn offers a range of family-friendly activities that are sure to keep both children and adults entertained. From wildlife encounters to thrilling adventures, here are some popular attractions for families in Tallinn:

Tallinn Zoo

Located in the beautiful surroundings of Veskimetsa Park, Tallinn Zoo is a must-visit for animal lovers. The zoo is home to a wide variety of animals from around the world, including elephants, lions, giraffes, penguins, and many more. The zoo focuses on providing a natural and spacious environment for the animals, ensuring an educational and enjoyable experience for visitors. In addition to observing the animals, you can also attend daily shows, educational talks, and feeding sessions.

Lennusadam Kids' Area

Lennusadam, or the Seaplane Harbour, is a maritime museum that offers an interactive and engaging experience for children. The museum's kids' area features hands-on exhibits, simulators, and games that allow children to learn about maritime history, navigation, and the mechanics of ships. Kids can try their hand at operating a submarine, steering a ship, or exploring a shipwreck. Lennusadam also houses an impressive collection of historical vessels, including a submarine and seaplanes, which can be explored.

Nõmme Adventure Park

For a day filled with outdoor adventures, head to Nõmme Adventure Park. Located in the Nõmme district of Tallinn, this park offers various activities suitable for both children and adults. The park features rope courses, ziplines, climbing walls, and other thrilling obstacles set among the trees. It's a great opportunity for the whole family to challenge themselves, test their skills, and enjoy an adrenaline-pumping experience amidst nature. The courses are designed with different difficulty levels, ensuring there's something for everyone, regardless of age or experience.

These family-friendly attractions in Tallinn provide opportunities for fun, learning, and quality time together. Whether you're exploring the diverse animal kingdom at Tallinn Zoo, engaging in interactive maritime experiences at Lennusadam, or embarking on outdoor adventures at Nõmme Adventure Park, you're sure to create lasting memories for the whole family.

CHAPTER 11:

SPORTS AND

RECREATION

Tallinn offers a range of sports and recreational activities for enthusiasts of all ages and interests. Whether you're a fan of water activities, winter sports, or golf, here are some options to consider:

Water Activities and Beaches

Tallinn's proximity to the Baltic Sea makes it an excellent destination for water activities and beach lovers. The city has several beaches where you can relax, swim, or engage in various water sports. Pirita Beach, located in the Pirita district, is one of the most popular beaches in Tallinn. It features a long sandy coastline and provides opportunities for swimming, sunbathing, beach volleyball, and windsurfing.

In addition to beach activities, you can also explore the coastal areas of Tallinn by renting a kayak, paddleboard, or taking a boat tour. The coastline offers picturesque views and the chance to discover hidden coves, small islands, and the beauty of Estonia's nature.

Skiing and Winter Sports

During the winter months, Tallinn transforms into a winter sports paradise. Just a short drive away from the city, you'll find various ski resorts where you can enjoy downhill skiing, snowboarding, and cross-country skiing. Popular ski resorts near Tallinn include Otepää, Kõrvemaa, and

Nõmmeveski. These resorts offer well-groomed slopes, rental equipment, and ski schools for beginners.

If you prefer a different kind of winter activity, you can also try ice skating. Tallinn has several ice rinks where you can glide across the ice and enjoy a fun-filled day with family and friends.

Golf Courses and Sports Facilities

Tallinn boasts several golf courses for golf enthusiasts. Niitvälja Golf, located just outside the city, is one of the oldest and most prestigious golf courses in Estonia. It offers a challenging 18-hole course set amidst beautiful natural surroundings. Estonian Golf & Country Club is another notable golf destination, featuring two championship-level courses and excellent practice facilities.

In addition to golf, Tallinn offers a range of sports facilities where you can engage in activities such as tennis, swimming, fitness, and team sports. Many sports centers and gyms provide various classes and equipment for both locals and visitors.

Tallinn provides ample opportunities for sports and recreation, whether you're looking to enjoy water activities at the beach, hit the slopes for winter sports, or tee off at a scenic golf course. With a combination of natural landscapes and well-equipped sports facilities, you can indulge in your favorite sports and leisure activities throughout the year.

CHAPTER 12:

TALLINN'S NIGHTLIFE

Tallinn offers a vibrant and diverse nightlife scene, with something to suit every taste. Whether you prefer relaxing in cozy bars, enjoying live music performances, or dancing the night away in energetic nightclubs, here are some highlights of Tallinn's nightlife:

Bars and Pubs

Tallinn is home to a wide variety of bars and pubs, offering a relaxed and laid-back atmosphere for socializing and enjoying a drink. The Old Town is particularly known for its charming bars tucked away in historic buildings and alleyways. Here, you can find cozy pubs with an extensive selection of craft beers, cocktails, and local spirits. Some bars also feature live music or DJ performances, creating a lively ambiance.

Telliskivi Creative City is another hotspot for bars, where you can find trendy and hip establishments serving craft beers, unique cocktails, and a wide range of beverages. The area often hosts events and themed nights, making it an exciting destination for a night out.

Live Music Venues

Tallinn boasts a vibrant live music scene, with venues that cater to various genres and tastes. From intimate jazz clubs to larger concert halls, you can find live performances throughout the city. The Von Krahl Theatre and Clazz are popular venues for jazz and blues enthusiasts, showcasing both local and international talent. Kultuurikatel, a former power plant turned cultural hub, hosts concerts and music events featuring a diverse range of genres.

For a more intimate setting, the piano bars in the Old Town offer a cozy atmosphere where you can enjoy live piano performances while sipping on your favorite drink. Many bars and cafes also feature occasional live music acts, providing a pleasant backdrop for an evening out.

Nightclubs and Dancing

If you're in the mood for dancing and energetic nightlife, Tallinn has a selection of nightclubs that cater to different music preferences. The nightlife district around the Viru Gate in the Old Town offers a concentration of clubs and venues, playing a variety of music genres such as electronic, pop, and mainstream hits. These clubs often feature international DJs and themed parties, ensuring an exciting and energetic atmosphere.

For a more alternative and underground scene, the Telliskivi Creative City hosts clubs that focus on electronic music and experimental sounds. These venues often have a more intimate setting and a dedicated following of electronic music enthusiasts.

It's important to note that Tallinn's nightlife scene may have specific age restrictions and entrance policies, so it's advisable to check the requirements and opening hours of each venue before planning your night out.

Tallinn's nightlife caters to a diverse range of preferences, offering an array of bars, live music venues, and nightclubs. Whether you're seeking a relaxed evening in a cozy pub, enjoying live music performances, or dancing until the early hours, Tallinn has plenty to offer for a memorable night out.

CHAPTER 13:

SUSTAINABLE TOURISM IN TALLINN

Tallinn is not only a beautiful and historic city but is also committed to sustainable tourism practices. The city has implemented various eco-friendly initiatives, preserved its parks and green spaces, and encourages responsible travel. Here are some highlights of sustainable tourism in Tallinn:

Eco-Friendly Practices and Initiatives

Tallinn has taken several measures to promote sustainable tourism and reduce its environmental impact. The city has implemented waste management systems that encourage recycling and responsible disposal of waste. You will find recycling bins throughout the city, so be sure to separate your waste accordingly.

Furthermore, Tallinn promotes the use of public transportation, cycling, and walking as eco-friendly modes of getting around.

The city has an efficient and well-connected public transportation system, including buses, trams, and trolleys, which makes it easy to explore the city without relying on private vehicles. Consider using a Tallinn Card, which provides unlimited access to public transportation and various attractions, further reducing your carbon footprint.

Parks and Green Spaces

Tallinn takes pride in its well-maintained parks and green spaces, offering residents and visitors a chance to connect with nature and enjoy the outdoors. Kadriorg Park, located in the heart of the city, is a prime example. The park features beautiful gardens, walking paths, and scenic spots where you can relax and appreciate the surrounding greenery. Strolling through the park is a delightful way to escape the hustle and bustle of the city.

Parks like Hirvepark and Toompark also offer tranquil spaces where you can have a picnic, play sports, or simply enjoy the fresh air. Tallinn's commitment to preserving and maintaining these green spaces enhances the city's overall sustainability and contributes to the well-being of both locals and visitors.

Responsible Travel Tips

To support sustainable tourism in Tallinn, consider practicing responsible travel during your visit. Here are a few tips to keep in mind:

a) **Conserve energy and water:** Make a conscious effort to turn off lights and appliances when not in use and limit your water consumption.

b) **Respect nature and wildlife:** When visiting parks and natural areas, follow designated trails, refrain from littering, and avoid disturbing wildlife.

c) **Support local businesses:** Choose locally owned restaurants, shops, and accommodations to support the local economy and reduce carbon emissions associated with long supply chains.

d) **Reduce plastic waste:** Carry a reusable water bottle and shopping bag, and opt for eco-friendly alternatives to single-use plastics whenever possible.

e) **Learn about local customs and traditions:** Respect the local culture and customs, and engage with locals in a friendly and culturally sensitive manner.

By adopting these responsible travel practices, you can contribute to the preservation of Tallinn's natural beauty and cultural heritage, ensuring that future generations can continue to enjoy the city's charms.

In conclusion, Tallinn is committed to sustainable tourism practices and offers various initiatives to promote eco-friendly travel. From implementing waste management systems to preserving parks and green spaces, the city strives to maintain its natural beauty while minimizing its environmental impact. By practicing responsible travel and supporting these efforts, you can contribute to the preservation of Tallinn's charm and ensure a sustainable future for the city and its visitors.

CHAPTER 14:

CALENDAR OF EVENTS
(for the year 2023)

Tallinn hosts a vibrant calendar of events throughout the year, showcasing its cultural richness, artistic expression, and sporting prowess. Whether you're interested in festivals, cultural events, or sports competitions, here are some highlights to look forward to in 2023:

Major Festivals and Celebrations

a) **Tallinn Music Week (March):** This annual music festival brings together local and international artists, offering a diverse range of genres and performances. From live concerts to industry conferences, Tallinn Music Week celebrates the city's music scene.

b) **Tallinn Old Town Days (June):** This festival takes place in the historic heart of the city and celebrates Tallinn's cultural heritage. Visitors can enjoy medieval-themed events, concerts, street performances, craft markets, and guided tours.

c) **Tallinn Maritime Days (July):** Celebrating the city's maritime history, this festival offers a variety of activities both on land and at sea. You can enjoy sailing regattas, ship parades, concerts, and delicious seafood.

d) **Birgitta Festival (August):** Held in the ruins of the Pirita Convent, this international festival showcases opera, musicals, and concerts. It attracts renowned performers and offers a unique cultural experience.

Cultural and Art Events

a)**Tallinn Photomonth (September-October):** This contemporary photography biennial features exhibitions, workshops, and discussions exploring different aspects of photography and visual culture.

b) **Tallinn Architecture Biennale (September-October):** The biennial event focuses on architectural innovation and urban development, offering exhibitions, installations, and lectures.

c) **Tallinn Black Nights Film Festival (November):** Known as PÖFF, this renowned film festival presents a diverse program of international and Estonian films, including feature films, documentaries, and shorts.

d) **Christmas Market (December):** As the holiday season approaches, Tallinn's Christmas Market transforms Town Hall Square into a winter wonderland. Visitors can enjoy festive decorations, local crafts, traditional food, and live performances.

Sports Events and Competitions

a) **Tallinn Marathon (September):** This annual running event attracts participants from around the world. With various race distances available, including a full marathon, half marathon, and 10K, it offers a scenic route through the city.

b) **Tallinn Cup (June):** As one of the largest youth football tournaments in Northern Europe, the Tallinn Cup brings together young football teams from different countries for a week of competitive matches.

c) **Tallinn Chess Festival (July):** Chess enthusiasts can witness high-level chess competitions and take part in open tournaments. The festival attracts both local and international chess players.

Please note that the exact dates and details of these events may vary each year, so it's advisable to check the official websites or local event listings for the most up-to-date information.

Tallinn's calendar of events offers a rich tapestry of cultural, artistic, and sporting experiences throughout the year. Whether you're a music lover, art enthusiast, or sports fan, these events provide an opportunity to immerse yourself in the city's vibrant cultural scene and celebrate its diverse offerings.

CONCLUSION AND FINAL THOUGHT

Tallinn is a captivating destination that effortlessly blends history, culture, and natural beauty. As you explore the charming streets of the Old Town, you'll be transported back in time, surrounded by medieval architecture and enchanting cobblestone lanes. The city's rich history and cultural significance are evident in its landmarks, museums, and festivals, providing visitors with a deep appreciation for its heritage.

Beyond the Old Town, Tallinn offers a modern and dynamic atmosphere. The city has embraced sustainable practices, preserving its parks and green spaces while promoting eco-friendly initiatives. Tallinn's commitment to sustainability enhances the overall visitor experience and contributes to the city's long-term well-being.

The culinary scene in Tallinn is a delightful fusion of traditional Estonian dishes, international flavors, and innovative gastronomy. From indulging in hearty meals to exploring local markets and savoring craft beers, Tallinn's dining options cater to all tastes and preferences.

Tallinn's proximity to various day trip destinations adds to its appeal. Whether you choose to venture to Helsinki, explore the natural wonders of Lahemaa National Park, or visit the picturesque Saaremaa Island, you'll find diverse experiences within easy reach of the city.

Practical information for visitors, such as transportation options and accommodation choices, ensures a seamless and enjoyable stay in Tallinn. The city's efficient public transportation system, coupled with a range of accommodation options, caters to the needs and preferences of all travelers.

Tallinn's calendar of events adds vibrancy and excitement throughout the year. From major festivals and celebrations to cultural and art events, there is always something happening in the city. Sports enthusiasts can also find their fill of excitement with various competitions and tournaments held throughout the year.

In conclusion, Tallinn offers a remarkable travel experience that combines history, culture, nature, and sustainability. Whether you're a history buff, a food lover, an art enthusiast, or an adventure seeker, Tallinn has something to offer everyone. Its unique blend of old-world charm and modernity creates an enchanting atmosphere that leaves a lasting impression on visitors. So pack your bags and embark on a journey to discover the wonders of Tallinn, where the past and present seamlessly coexist.

Printed in Great Britain
by Amazon